My Friend Jesus

Jennifer Ann Barton

Grosvenor House
Publishing Limited

The right of Jennifer Ann Barton to be identified as the author of this
work has been asserted in accordance with Section 78
of the Copyright, Designs and Patents Act 1988

The book cover is copyright to Jennifer Ann Barton

This book is published by
Grosvenor House Publishing Ltd
Link House
140 The Broadway, Tolworth, Surrey, KT6 7HT.
www.grosvenorhousepublishing.co.uk

A CIP record for this book
is available from the British Library

ISBN 978-1-83615-040-4

Dedication

This book is dedicated to my darling mother Pauline Mifsud who loved me so tenderly, and helped me to love the Lord, and walk in his ways.

Also, to my beloved animals and husband Mike for their constant love.

Acknowledgement

I would like to thank my dear husband, Mike Barton, for his help and encouragement to produce my books.

Introduction

Dear children, I wanted to tell you my story about Jesus because he has been a good friend to me.

He is in all things, and his spirit is like the wind that blows. No one can see it, but it is everywhere all around, you can feel it.

Jesus is very special; he is the son of God and has a lot of power.

You must remember he is a being of light and love, and he gave up his life so that all the bad things we do will be forgiven.

I hope that this book will start you on your journey.

xxx

Contents

The Winter Story

2

My house is set on the edge of a little wood and is the place I love to be more than anywhere else.

There are six of us in my family, my mum and dad, two sisters and my baby brother. We also have some animals that we all love very much.

All of us kids went to a school near our home which had a church right next to it.

The service was in another language which my mum told me was Latin. It sounded so beautiful.

I used to daydream, gazing at the flame on the large candles, and there was a lovely smell that came from them.

I remember seeing a lady wearing a beautiful lace scarf on her head, I felt at peace as I knew the Lord Jesus was close.

One winter morning I noticed that thick snow had fallen overnight.

I looked out of the window filled with excitement.

Everything looked magical as I gazed into the distance at the wood. Every tree was covered in frosty snow, and there was a glow coming through the window.

I put on all of my warm clothes and asked my mum if I could go out. She said I could but not to go too far.

I rushed out of the door as the freezing air almost took my breath away.

As young as I was, only seven years old, I trusted Jesus and I loved him just like one of my family. I had been taught about him and prayed to him often. He became my friend.

As soon as I stood in the wood seeing the snowflakes fall softly from the trees it reminded me of icing dripping from a cake and I thought Christmas will soon be here!

I walked further into the wood which looked so beautiful, and I began to sing a song to Jesus about how wonderful nature was. I was so very happy.

Then the snow started falling again and the wind started blowing.

I could not see where I was going as the snow swirled around me.

After walking around for quite a while, I realized I was lost, and my heart started pounding. I had wandered too far. I turned my head in every direction trying to remember which way I came from. I began to feel lost and alone and very frightened and I began to cry.

I thought about asking Jesus to help me to find my way back home. I knew if I asked him, he would help me. So, I dried my tears away and asked in prayer. "Dear Jesus, please, please, help me find my way back home."

I was so afraid and upset that my mum would be worried about me.

Suddenly I felt something tapping my leg and when I looked down, I saw a white rabbit.

It was so white I thought it might be an angel!

He suddenly ran off running very fast and I knew I needed to follow him. I felt sure he was sent to help me find my way home.

I ran through the deep snow which was up to my knees and the cold began to start getting through my clothes.

I called out to the rabbit to slow down but he just kept going. He ran so fast that I sometimes thought he was flying.

I suddenly lost my footing and fell face-first into the snow.

I struggled to my feet; I had no feeling in my hands now as they were so cold. I looked around and in front of me and I could see the white rabbit ahead of me.

I ran and ran until I realized I was coming out of the wood, and I saw my house with smoke coming from the chimney being blown about in the wild wind.

I was overcome with relief as I used the last of my energy to run toward my house. I could hear my dear mother calling.

"Jenny, Jenny!"

I ran into her arms. I felt warm and loved once more. I was home thanks to Jesus sending the little rabbit angel to help me.

The Spring Story

As the days grew longer and the birds sang louder, I felt excited by the way things in nature were changing. I walked across the meadows on a fresh spring morning taking a deep breath.

The air was filled with the scent of spring flowers and fresh grass.

The birds sounded so happy and I felt that way too.

I thanked Jesus for the beauty all around me and for such a special loving family. I skipped off singing the song *Morning has broken* … "Morning has broken like the first morning" …

The sun and the fresh air made my face tingle and I felt so alive!

The spirit of Jesus was around everywhere!

I went and sat at the foot of a huge oak tree and looked up to the very top. I saw how the branches reached up to the deep blue sky like arms reaching out to a heavenly place above.

Then suddenly I heard some birds making really loud noises and when I looked down I saw a bird resting on the ground, he was crying for his mother and I felt so sad. Then I heard some rustling noises, and when I looked across I saw two very large green eyes staring at the helpless baby on the ground.

It was a hungry cat ready to pounce.

I ran and chased off the cat but I knew he would be back as soon as I was gone. There was only one thing to do that was to pick up the bird and take him home to my loving mum who had fed birds before with such gentleness and love.

So I picked up the baby bird and ran home back through the wood whilst he wriggled in my hands.

Then the words came to me that the Father in heaven, the creator of all things knows even when a small bird is injured or dies.

Jesus is the only son of God, so he knows all things.

As I ran through the garden I shouted … "Mum! Mum! I found a baby bird and a cat nearly got him. Can you help me look after him until he gets bigger?"

My mum came toward me and I handed her the bird.

"You have to be careful about picking up wild birds because they may be rejected by their mother when you put them back," she said softly.

"I only picked him up because he was about to be killed by a cat," I explained.

"Okay we will see what we can do," said my mum looking for something to put the bird in.

Every day me and my mum fed the bird and gave him water, and he kept popping his head up to see what we were doing. That made me laugh.

A few days went by and I thought I would ask Jesus to make sure the little bird gets big and strong and can fly through the air. I prayed so hard for him.

I sat in the sparkling sunlight imagining the bird flying high with his mum, brothers and sisters.

Then one day after school I went to check on the baby bird but he was laying down perfectly still. I touched his little head but he did not move.

"Mum!" I called starting to cry. "The bird is not moving."

My mum rushed over to the little box hanging in the window and said, "Jenny, the little bird is dead".

"But how can that be, we took such good care of him and showed him so much love?"

I prayed and prayed for the little bird to be okay. Why did Jesus ignore my prayers? I sobbed.

Mum gave me a cuddle, and I felt her warmth and love, I felt safe again.

"But what about my friend Jesus," I said, "Why did he let the little bird die"?

My mum told me that we all have to die one day. But I still wondered why Jesus couldn't let the bird live his little life.

Of course, at such a young age it is hard to understand, it was one of the first things that happened to me that I found hard to accept in life.

Sometimes Jesus will not stop things from happening for a reason that we do not understand.

Life is like a very large puzzle with pieces that have to fit together. It is all part of his plan.

The Summer Story

Whenever Summer came it seemed as if there were a lot of small planes flying through the blue sky making a soothing humming sound.

One warm summer's day I lay in the back garden on the soft grass with the sun shining on my face. I thought about my friend Jesus and how he died for us all so that when we die, we will not be gone forever. I was filled with love and was so thankful.

Then suddenly, I heard the sound of loud crying which made me jump to my feet. I tried to work out which direction the sound was coming from. I jumped over the fence and looked around the field, which looked lovely as it was covered in daisies and buttercups. I then saw a little boy and he was crying so much.

I saw some other children running away with the little boy's toys.

I thought, what would Jesus do in this situation? This is what I was taught to do. I raced over to him and shouted out to the bullies as they ran away.

I put my arm around the little boy and dried his tears with a tissue. His eyes were red and swollen, I felt so sorry for him, I told him I would be his friend forever.

We walked past the bullies who were now shouting. I held the little boy's arm and we walked away to my house. Once there I sat him in the garden on a blanket which had been warmed by the hot sun and ran into the kitchen.

"Mum, see that little boy, he has been crying so much because he has been teased by bullies and had his toys stolen."

"Get him a cup of tea darling and take some of these cakes out to him and put them on the table. It might cheer him up," she said gently.

I quickly got some delicious cakes and some drinks my mum had made, walked out into the sunny garden and placed them on the table that was already set for teatime.

The birds were singing so loudly, and I could smell the flowers in the air and the fresh washing on the line.

We both sat on a tree stump, and I could see the little boy was calmer now.

"What is your name, little boy?" I asked quietly.

"My name is Jimmy, those boys keep calling me names," he said sadly.

"Oh, don't take any notice — they are just very stupid," I said.

I passed him a drink and cakes, and as his eyes dried, he began to smile.

As his eyes glistened in the sunlight, I started to pray to Jesus asking him to keep Jimmy safe when he leaves the garden, and I asked Jesus if I had done all of the right things. As I did this, I felt so peaceful like I was floating, I felt love all around us. That was my reward for doing what Jesus would have done.

As the sun shone and the sky grew ever bluer, we started to play and laugh together.

The long summer holidays stretched out before me, and I was excited that I was going to spend a lot of time with my mum.

As I said goodbye to Jimmy my mum called me, "Jenny, is Jimmy okay now?"

"Yes, he is happy now, I treated him just as Jesus would have and it has changed his whole day."

We hugged each other and I thanked God for my mum.

I went and sat on a swing I had made from a curtain on the washing line, and I fell fast asleep in the warm sunshine. I had a dream about Jesus holding a staff, a long piece of wood with a large hook on the end, like a walking stick. The hook is for the shepherds who look after the sheep to hook them around the neck when they stray so that they do not get lost.

In many pictures of Jesus, he is holding a staff because it means not only that he would protect the sheep, but it stands for the protection, comfort and love he has for us all. He brings back those who get too far away from him.

I went and sat on a wooden fence facing the fields and felt happy that I had pleased Jesus with the way I lived my life. But I could sense a change in the air, Autumn was on its way.

The Autumn Story

I woke early one morning, and although the sunlight was very weak, the colours of the leaves were so beautiful. I had gone to the front door and watched the leaves falling, one by one, from the trees. Slowly, slowly, through the cool air.

Even though everything looked lovely, I could not help but notice a loss in nature as things were beginning to die.

Later that day I sat at my mum's feet and watched her writing a letter to her dear mum far away over the seas on the little island of Malta.

I watched her face to see what she was thinking. Then suddenly a tear dripped down on to the page.

"Don't cry mummy, please don't cry," I said holding her hand.

She told me there would be a time when we would not be separated any more. This is because Jesus gave up his life so that we can live all together again in Heaven one day.

When the letter was written I asked my mum why the Summer has to end, and she told me that everything has its time … a time for living and a time for dying, a time for sadness and a time for joy.

I wandered off into the garden trying to understand what my mum had told me.

As I sat on the soft grass watching the birds play, I realized there was no time to waste so I jumped to my feet and ran indoors and found a container. I went around the garden picking up the gold and red leaves from the ground. I knew I had to save as many as I could before the cold winter weather arrived. When I was finished, I picked the flowers that were left and went inside to get a vase. I filled it with water and put some large spoonfuls of sugar to feed the flowers.

My next job was to find food for all of the little animals who needed to stock up their food for the winter.

I pressed some leaves in books and then I went and collected lots of lovely things for the birds to eat. I put it all out into the garden on the edge of the wood. It was starting to get cold, but I had such a pretty dress on I did not want to cover it up.

I started to walk through the wood, and I saw berries in all different shades, and I thought about how beautiful nature is and that God had made all of it.

When I thought about this, I skipped back home singing. I picked handfuls of leaves in my hands and threw them in the air, knowing that everything will come to life again in the spring!